Sugar Glider

A Fun and Educational Book for Kids with Amazing Facts and Pictures

Table of Contents

Introduction

Little, nocturnal marsupials called sugar gliders are indigenous to Australia, Indonesia, and Papua New Guinea. They are known as sugar gliders because of the way a unique membrane that spreads between their front and rear legs allows them to float through the air.

The average length of a sugar glider is 6 inches, and their tail is about the same length as their body. They can live up to 15 years and weigh between 3 and 5 ounces. Being sociable creatures, they dwell in colonies of up to seven individuals in the wild.

Sugar gliders can be loving and entertaining pets when kept in captivity, but they need a lot of care and attention. They require a sizable cage with room to climb and play, a diet rich in different fruits and insects as well as a specially made pellet meal, and routine checks with a veterinarian.

Scientific Name

Petaurus breviceps is the sugar glider's scientific name.

Appearance

The bodies of sugar gliders are small and compact, and their silky, dense fur comes in a variety of colors, from gray to brown to black. Their ears are big and pointed, and they have big, round eyes.

Their gliding membrane, also known as a patagium, which spans from their front to hind legs and allows them to glide in the air, is one of their most remarkable characteristics. The membrane is covered in fur, and when it is extended, it forms a structure resembling a parachute that enables sugar gliders to fly up to 50 meters.

The average adult sugar glider is about 6 inches long, weighs 3 to 5 ounces, and has a tail that is about the same length as their body. Although males are marginally bigger than females, these differences are not very noticeable.

Geography

Sugar gliders can be found in a variety of environments, including forests, woodlands, and savannas, in their native countries of Australia, Indonesia, and Papua New Guinea.

Almost the whole Australian continent, with the exception of the arid central parts, is covered by sugar gliders. They are mostly found in the northern and eastern regions of Indonesia and Papua New Guinea.

Moreover, sugar gliders have been brought to other nations, particularly the United States, where they are frequently kept as pets. It is crucial to remember that some nations have laws governing the importation and ownership of sugar gliders as pets, and in other situations, doing so is against the law.

Behavior

Sugar gliders are sociable creatures with a reputation for being fun and active. They can live in colonies of up to seven people in the wild, where they coexist. They use vocalizations, scent marking, and body language to communicate with one another.

The ability of sugar gliders to soar through the air is among their most amazing actions. They can cover up to 50 meters between trees by leaping between them using their gliding membrane. Being skilled climbers, sugar gliders can easily scale trees and other tall surfaces.

Animals that are nocturnal, or active at night and sleeping during the day, include sugar gliders. They require a lot of toys and entertainment in captivity to keep them entertained, and they benefit from having a friend.

Sugar gliders are omnivores, which means they consume both plants and animals in their diet. They consume nectar, fruit, insects, and tiny creatures like spiders and lizards in the wild. They require a variety of foods, such as fruits, vegetables, insects, and a specially made pellet food, when living in captivity.

Reproduction

Sugar gliders have an unusual method of reproduction. Males have a bifurcated penis, whereas females have two uteri and two vagina. This means that since each embryo develops in a different uterus, ladies are capable of giving birth to twins.

Changes in temperature and daylight hours have an impact on sugar glider mating, which normally takes place between July and January in the southern hemisphere.

The female gives birth to joeys that are around the size of a grain of rice after a gestation period of about 16 days. During roughly two to three months, the joeys will continue to grow in the mother's pouch. During this time, they will eat the mother's milk.

The young will remain with their parents for several weeks after emerging from the pouch and suckle until they are about six months old. Sugar gliders can live up to 15 years in captivity and attain sexual maturity at a young age of 8 to 12 months.

Social Life

In the wild, sugar gliders live in communities known as colonies. Up to seven individuals can make up a normal colony, and they interact with one another by using a range of vocalizations, scent marking, and body language.

Sugar gliders need social connection with their keepers or other gliders when they are in captivity. They are renowned for developing close relationships with their owners, but they also gain from having a comrade from a different species. Maintaining a group of sugar gliders needs appropriate socializing and introductions, as well as giving each glider with enough room and resources to survive.

When housed in groups, sugar gliders will frequently groom and sleep near to one another in a common nest. It can be fun to see them play together while climbing and gliding through their surroundings.

Although they can be loving and entertaining pets, sugar gliders need a lot of care and attention, and their social needs must be satisfied to maintain their wellbeing.

Habitat

Sugar gliders are indigenous to Australia, Indonesia, and Papua New Guinea's forests, woodlands, and savannas. They are adapted to living in a variety of forest settings, from tropical rainforests to temperate eucalyptus forests, as they are arboreal animals who spend the most of their time in trees.

In the wild, sugar gliders fly between trees and explore their surroundings using their gliding membrane. They create their nests in cracks or hollows in trees, and they mark their territory with urine.

Sugar gliders need a large habitat in captivity with lots of options for climbing and soaring. In order to replicate their natural habitat, the cage should be provided with branches, ropes, and other objects. For the gliders to rest during the day, it's essential to provide hiding places like nest boxes or pouches.

Sugar gliders also need a warm, humid environment with temperatures between 75 and 90 degrees Fahrenheit (24 and

32 degrees Celsius) and humidity levels between 50 and 70 percent. The right lighting is also necessary because sugar gliders need to be exposed to natural light to stay healthy and happy.

Senses

Sugar gliders have highly developed senses that aid in locating food and navigating their surroundings. They have the following senses:

Vision: Sugar gliders can see better at night, when they are most active, thanks to their big, rounded eyes that are optimized for low light situations. In order to glide through trees, they must also have good depth awareness.

Hearing: Sugar gliders have keen hearing and can pick up high-frequency noises that are inaudible to humans. They can find insects and other nighttime prey thanks to this.

Smell: Sugar gliders have a keen sense of smell, which they employ for both locating food and communication. On their forehead and breast, they have smell glands that they utilize to communicate with other gliders and mark their territory.

Touch: Sugar gliders can navigate their environment and locate food because to their sensitive whiskers and highly developed sense of touch.

Taste: Sugar gliders have taste buds on their tongues and in their mouths, which aids in their ability to recognize various flavors and choose healthy things to eat.

In general, sugar gliders use their senses to explore their surroundings and interact with other gliders. Their senses are critical to their behavior and social interactions, as well as to their ability to survive in the wild.

Feeding

In the environment, sugar gliders consume a wide range of foods, including nectar, sap, insects, fruit, and small vertebrates. They are omnivores. They require a balanced diet in captivity that offers all the nutrients necessary for optimum health.

A sugar glider kept in captivity should eat the following foods:

a premium commercial pellet food created especially for sugar gliders.

Fruits and vegetables that are still in season, such apples, grapes, sweet potatoes, and carrots.

insects as a source of protein, including mealworms and crickets.

commercially available goodies, such as meal replacement

powders or yogurt drops, designed especially for sugar gliders.

Foods heavy in sugar, fat, or salt should not be fed to sugar gliders as they can lead to health issues like obesity, diabetes, and heart disease. Sugar gliders may also develop dental issues as a result of eating sugary foods.

A shallow dish or a water bottle should always be available to provide sugar gliders with fresh, clean water.

Overall, providing sugar gliders with a well-balanced food is crucial for maintaining their health and wellbeing, and their diet should be customized to fit their individual nutritional requirements.

Diet

Sugar gliders are omnivores, which means that in the wild, they consume both plant-based and animal-based diets. To preserve their health and avoid nutritional deficits while in captivity, they need a diet rich in protein, fiber, and vitamins.

For sugar gliders kept in captivity, a balanced diet should include the following:

Pellets of commercial food created especially for sugar gliders: They should eat a lot of this since it contains important elements including protein, fiber, and vitamins.

Fresh fruits and vegetables, such as apples, bananas, papayas, carrots, and leafy greens, should be offered to children every day. They supply minerals, vitamins, and fiber.

Protein: A source of protein, such as cooked chicken, boiled eggs, mealworms, crickets, or other insects, should be offered to sugar gliders at least twice a week.

Treats: Moderate amounts of commercial sugar glider snacks, like yogurt drops or dried fruit, can be given on occasion.

Foods heavy in fat, sugar, or salt should not be fed to sugar gliders as they can lead to health issues like obesity, diabetes, and heart disease. Sugar gliders may also develop dental issues as a result of eating sugary foods.

Sugar gliders should always have access to fresh, clean water, either through a water bottle or a shallow dish.

Overall, feeding sugar gliders in captivity a balanced, diverse diet is crucial for their health and wellbeing. To make sure that your sugar glider is eating a nutritionally balanced food, you should speak with a veterinarian or animal nutritionist.

Babies

Sugar gliders are sexually receptive, and females normally produce litters of one to two young, known as joeys. From 16 to 21 days pass during gestation.

The joeys are underdeveloped when they are born, and they spend the following 70 to 80 days in their mother's pouch, where they grow and suckle. The mother will tend to and guard her young throughout this time, and she will take them wherever she goes.

Following their exit from the pouch, the joeys will nurse for a number of weeks before beginning to eat solid food. By the time they are 10 to 12 weeks old, they will be completely weaned, and by the time they are 6 to 8 months old, they will be sexually mature.

It is significant to note that sugar gliders demand a great deal of care and attention during their formative years, and it is not advised to breed them without the necessary skills and understanding. Also, if you're thinking about getting a sugar glider as a pet, you should be sure to buy it from a reputable breeder to make sure it has been well-taken care of and is healthy.

Predators

Little creatures called sugar gliders have a variety of natural predators in the wild. Sugar gliders are frequently preyed upon by hawks and owls, as well as by snakes, foxes, and feral cats.

Many changes made by sugar gliders aid in their ability to elude predators. Due to their nocturnal nature, they are most active at night, when many predators are sleeping. They may readily flee danger by climbing up trees and gliding away because they are also adept climbers.

In addition to their natural predators, domestic cats and dogs who are kept as pets may pose a threat to sugar gliders. By giving sugar gliders a safe enclosure and keeping an eye on them when they venture outside of it, you can keep them safe.

Therefore, despite the fact that sugar gliders have a number of adaptations that aid in their ability to evade predators, it is crucial to keep them safe and secure when they are kept in captivity to avoid harm or even death at the hands of domestic animals.

Evolution

The family Petauridae, which also comprises a number of species of small, gliding marsupials, includes sugar gliders. The earliest petaurid marsupial fossils were discovered in the Oligocene period, some 34 million years ago.

Around 15 million years ago, during the Miocene period, when Australia and New Guinea were becoming more segregated from other land masses, the evolution of sugar gliders is assumed to have started. The ability to glide from tree to tree and their capacity to eat a range of things, including nectar, insects, and small animals, are only two of the specialized adaptations sugar gliders have developed over time to survive and thrive in their particular environment.

Even though sugar gliders have been kept as pets for a long time, in recent years their appeal as pets has grown, which has prompted further study into their biology, behavior, and evolution. Sugar gliders should only be maintained as pets by people who are prepared to give them the right care and surroundings, however, as they are wild animals that need a lot of attention and care.

Population

Since sugar gliders are nocturnal, elusive, and challenging to monitor, it is challenging to estimate their population in the wild. They are not thought to be a threatened or endangered species as a whole because they are common throughout their native range in Australia and New Guinea.

Nonetheless, the number of sugar gliders kept in captivity has grown recently, notably as pets. While dedicated owners of sugar gliders may find them to be entertaining and fulfilling, it's vital to keep in mind that these exotic creatures have specific demands and should only be kept by people who can provide them the care and attention they need. Also, it's critical to buy sugar gliders from trustworthy breeders who put the wellbeing and health of their animals first.

Conservation Status

The International Union for Conservation of Nature (IUCN) has classified sugar gliders as having a conservation category of "Least Concern," which means that the species is not currently thought to be in danger of going extinct.

It is crucial to remember, nevertheless, that habitat loss brought on by deforestation, as well as habitat fragmentation brought on by agriculture and urbanization, can have a detrimental effect on populations of sugar gliders. Also, certain locations where sugar gliders are found have been exposed to introduced predators like foxes and feral cats, which may pose a threat to them.

Sugar gliders are occasionally killed for their meat or for use in traditional medicines in some areas. Even while hunting is typically not regarded as posing a serious threat to the species, it is crucial to make sure that it is handled responsibly and does not have a harmful effect on nearby populations.

Thus, despite the fact that sugar gliders are not currently

thought to be in danger of going extinct, human activities can have an impact on their populations, so it is crucial to keep an eye on them and take precautions to safeguard both them and their habitats.

Health

When given the right care and surroundings, sugar gliders are generally healthy animals. Yet, they are prone to a range of health problems, just like any animals.

Obesity, which can result in a number of health conditions, including as diabetes and heart disease, is one of the most prevalent health problems in sugar gliders. A healthy, diverse diet as well as lots of opportunity for exercise are essential for sugar gliders.

Moreover, sugar gliders are susceptible to dental abnormalities including enlarged teeth, which can make it challenging for them to consume and result in other health concerns. Dental cleanings and routine veterinarian exams can help avoid dental issues.

Infections of the respiratory system, parasites, and wounds sustained in slips or battles with other animals are other typical health problems in sugar gliders. To assist prevent and handle health issues, it's crucial to give sugar gliders a clean and secure habitat in addition to regular medical care.

Finding a trustworthy veterinarian with experience treating sugar gliders is crucial if you are thinking about getting a sugar glider as a pet. Your sugar glider's health and happiness can be supported by routine veterinarian exams.

Lifespan

Although the sugar glider's life expectancy in the wild is not fully known, it is thought that they typically survive for 5-7 years. With the right care and attention, sugar gliders can live for up to 12–15 years in captivity.

Diet, exercise, environmental factors, and veterinary treatment can all have an impact on a sugar glider's longevity. Sugar gliders can have a long and healthy life if given a nutritious diet that is balanced, numerous opportunities for play and exercise, a clean and secure living space, and routine veterinary treatment.

It's crucial to keep in mind that caring for sugar gliders is a lengthy commitment that requires a lot of time and effort. Research the care requirements of sugar gliders before acquiring one as a pet to be sure you can meet those demands for the duration of the animal's life.

Conclusion

Finally, it should be noted that sugar gliders are unusual and intriguing creatures that are found only in Australia and New Guinea. These are tiny, nocturnal marsupials that can glide, and they have an outgoing, gregarious attitude.

Although sugar gliders as a species are not regarded as threatened or endangered, habitat degradation, hunting, and imported predators can have an impact on their populations. Sugar gliders can be entertaining and gratifying pets, but they need a lot of care and attention to thrive.

Sugar gliders can have a long and healthy life if given a balanced diet, lots of opportunity for play and exercise, a clean and secure living space, and routine veterinary care. We can appreciate these unusual creatures and help to protect them and their environments if we comprehend and respect the needs of sugar gliders.

Thank you

CPSIA information can be obtained
at www.ICGtesting.com
Printed in the USA
LVHW071240150723
752574LV00039B/1287